W9-BZN-251

AMERICAN INDIANS AND AFRICAN AMERICANS OF THE AMERICAN REVOLUTION— THROUGH

PRIMARY SOURCES

John Micklos, Jr.

Enslow Publishers, Inc.
40 Industrial Road
Box 398
Berkeley Heights, NJ 07922
USA
http://www.enslow.com

Original edition published as *African Americans and American Indians Fighting in the Revolutionary War* in 2008.

Library of Congress Cataloging-in-Publication Data

Micklos, John.
  American Indians and African Americans of the American Revolution—through primary sources /
  John Micklos, Jr.
    pages cm. — (The American Revolution through primary sources)
  "Original edition published as African Americans and American Indians Fighting in the Revolutionary
  War in 2008."
  Includes bibliographical references and index.
  Summary: "Examines the lives and roles of African Americans and American Indians during the American
  Revolution, including the difficulty of choosing sides in the war and fighting for the Americans and the
  British"—Provided by publisher.
  ISBN 978-0-7660-4130-1
  1. United States—History—Revolution, 1775–1783—Participation, African American—Juvenile literature.
  2. United States—History—Revolution, 1775–1783—Participation, Indian—Juvenile literature. I. Title.
  E269.N3M53 2013
  973.3'8—dc23

          2012020817

Future editions:
Paperback ISBN 978-1-4644-0188-6
ePUB ISBN 978-1-4645-1101-1
PDF ISBN 978-1-4646-1101-8

Printed in the United States of America.

082012 Lake Book Manufacturing, Inc., Melrose Park, IL

10 9 8 7 6 5 4 3 2 1

To Our Readers: We have done our best to make sure all Internet Addresses in this book were active and appropriate when we went to press. However, the author and the publisher have no control over and assume no liability for the material available on those Internet sites or on other Web sites they may link to. Any comments or suggestions can be sent by email to comments@enslow.com or to the address on the back cover.

♻ Enslow Publishers, Inc., is committed to printing our books on recycled paper. The paper in every book contains 10% to 30% post-consumer waste (PCW). The cover board on the outside of each book contains 100% PCW. Our goal is to do our part to help young people and the environment too!

Illustration Credits: Colonial Williamsburg, p. 32; © Corel Corporation, p. 4; Domenick D'Andrea, courtesy of the National Guard, pp. 1, 5, 19, 34; Enslow Publishers, Inc., p. 8; The Granger Collection, NYC, pp. 17, 20, 39; Independence National Historical Park, p. 28; Library of Congress Prints and Photographs, pp. 3, 10, 13, 22, 26, 36; Library of Congress Prints and Photographs via Eon Images, p. 6; Library of Congress Rare Books and Special Collections, p. 24; U.S. Army Center of Military History, p. 30; Virginia Historical Society, p. 11.

Cover Illustration: Library of Congress (Crispus Attucks portrait) and Independence National Historical Park (Charles Willson Peale painting of Joseph Brant).

CONTENTS

LOOK FOR THIS SYMBOL **PRIMARY SOURCE** TO FIND THE PRIMARY SOURCES THROUGHOUT THIS BOOK.

Peter Salem, a black slave, was one of the first men to fire a shot during the American Revolution at the Battle of Lexington. He agreed to fight for the colonial militia in exchange for his freedom. Salem is shown here at the Battle of Bunker Hill. This image came from part of a 1786 John Trumbull painting depicting the battle.

CHAPTER 1

ON THE EVE OF THE REVOLUTION

Their bayonets gleamed in the early morning sun. On April 19, 1775, British soldiers marched into the town of Lexington, Massachusetts. There, they faced off against a colonial militia company. Soon, shots rang out. The fighting continued later in nearby Concord. The first shot that day became known as "the shot heard 'round the world." These battles marked the start of the American Revolution.

Like many of his friends, Peter Salem fired his musket at the British that day. Unlike most of the others, Salem was a slave. He had signed up for the militia because his master had promised him freedom if he did so.[1]

TO BE SOLD on board the Ship *Bance-Island*, on tuesday the 6th of *May* next, at *Ashley-Ferry*; a choice cargo of about 250 fine healthy

NEGROES,

just arrived from the Windward & Rice Coast. —The utmost care has already been taken, and shall be continued, to keep them free from the least danger of being infected with the SMALL-POX, no boat having been on board, and all other communication with people from *Charles-Town* prevented.

Austin, Laurens, & Appleby.

N. B. Full one Half of the above Negroes have had the SMALL-POX in their own Country.

This is a 1780s newspaper advertisement for the sale of slaves at Ashley Ferry near Charleston, South Carolina. The slave trade flourished in North America from the day the first slaves landed in 1619 into the nineteenth century.

In 1775, 2.5 million people lived in the thirteen colonies. Of this total, about one in five—or 500,000 people—were slaves.[2] Most of these slaves lived in the southern colonies. A much smaller number lived in the North.[3]

In 1619, about twenty black people had been brought aboard a ship to the British colony of Jamestown in Virginia. Scholars believe that these men, who were probably seized as slaves in southwestern Africa, were among the first blacks in America.

Over the following decades, thousands of black Africans were brought to the colonies as slaves. The long voyage across the Atlantic Ocean from Africa was brutal. Many slaves died during the trip.

Once in America, slaves lived a hard life. Most worked in the fields all day. They grew crops such as rice and tobacco.

Unequal Treatment

The Declaration of Independence stated that "all men are created equal."[4] In many cases, however, blacks were not treated as equals. Many of the Founding Fathers owned slaves. Even among the colonists who did not own slaves, most believed that black people were not as good as white people.

Many colonists did not think highly of American Indians, either. The Declaration of Independence called them "merciless Indian Savages."[5]

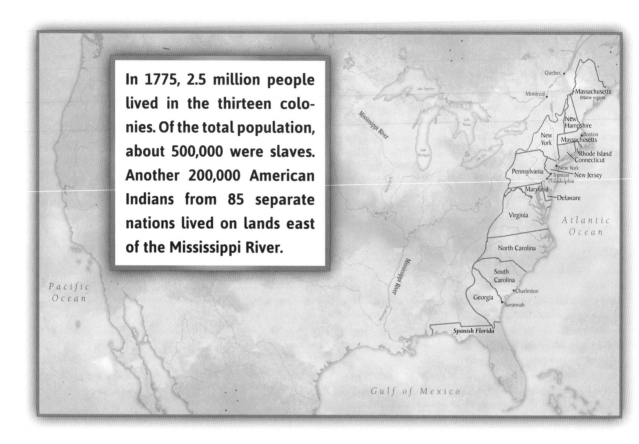

In 1775, 2.5 million people lived in the thirteen colonies. Of the total population, about 500,000 were slaves. Another 200,000 American Indians from 85 separate nations lived on lands east of the Mississippi River.

Slaves working in the Deep South tended to have harsher and shorter lives than slaves farther north.[6]

Most African Americans in the northern colonies did not live as slaves. A few in the South were free as well. They were able to hold jobs and own houses. Still, they did not enjoy the same rights as white people. Whites did not view them as equals.

Many whites also did not view American Indians as equals. At the start of the American Revolution, there were about 200,000 American Indians living east of the Mississippi River.[7] They came from 85 separate Indian nations. Most wanted to stay out of the conflict. They simply wanted to live in peace.

Still, the American Indians knew the war affected them. Many tribes fought with settlers who had moved onto their lands. These tribes wished to keep their lands. They wanted to preserve their way of life. With this in mind, most tribes sided with the British. They thought the British would help protect them from the land-hungry settlers.

As the war began, most blacks in America were slaves. Even those who were free lacked the rights that whites had. They hoped the war might somehow help them gain more rights. Meanwhile, American Indians feared losing their land and their way of life. They hoped the war might somehow help them preserve both.

CHAPTER 2

★

WHICH SIDE TO CHOOSE?

When the American Revolution began in 1775, colonists fought to protect their rights as English subjects. Most remained loyal to the king. By the next year, the focus had turned to liberty. The Declaration of Independence said it all. America wanted freedom from England. Nearly 500,000 slaves throughout the colonies wondered if the war might bring them freedom as well.

Few slaves found freedom before the war. Some were set free by their masters. A few managed to earn enough money to pay for their freedom. Many tried to escape. While some succeeded, most failed. Those who were captured faced harsh punishment.

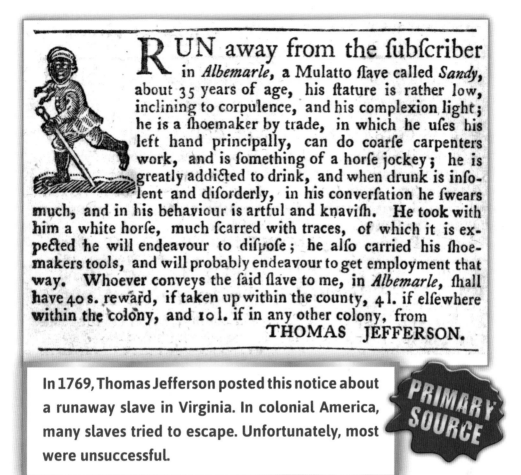

RUN away from the subscriber in *Albemarle*, a Mulatto slave called *Sandy*, about 35 years of age, his stature is rather low, inclining to corpulence, and his complexion light; he is a shoemaker by trade, in which he uses his left hand principally, can do coarse carpenters work, and is something of a horse jockey; he is greatly addicted to drink, and when drunk is insolent and disorderly, in his conversation he swears much, and in his behaviour is artful and knavish. He took with him a white horse, much scarred with traces, of which it is expected he will endeavour to dispose; he also carried his shoemakers tools, and will probably endeavour to get employment that way. Whoever conveys the said slave to me, in *Albemarle*, shall have 40 s. reward, if taken up within the county, 4 l. if elsewhere within the colony, and 10 l. if in any other colony, from
THOMAS JEFFERSON.

In 1769, Thomas Jefferson posted this notice about a runaway slave in Virginia. In colonial America, many slaves tried to escape. Unfortunately, most were unsuccessful.

PRIMARY SOURCE

Some slaves knew of a slave case that had been settled in England in 1772. In that case, a slave named James Sommersett had been purchased in Virginia. He was taken to England, where he escaped. He was later recaptured. The judge ruled that Sommersett could not be returned to his master against his will.[1] Other slaves reasoned that if they could get to England, they too could be free.

The First Martyr

Tensions ran high in Boston, Massachusetts, in early 1770. British troops occupied the city. That made the residents angry. On the evening of March 5, the anger led to violence. A crowd of patriots gathered around the British soldiers on duty.

The mob yelled insults and threw snowballs. The British soldiers raised their guns in defense. The crowd dared them to fire. Then a club flew through the air. It hit one of the soldiers. Soon, shots rang out. Three men near the front of the mob fell dead. Eight others were wounded. Two of them later died. The incident became known as the Boston Massacre.

One of the first to die was Crispus Attucks, who was part black and part American Indian. Attucks and the others who died were called martyrs. These are people who die to support a cause.

Crispus Attucks was the first man shot and killed during the Boston Massacre on March 5, 1770. Paul Revere depicted Attucks's death in his engraving of the incident titled "The Bloody Massacre Perpetrated in King's Street."

Washington's Plea

American leaders tried to win the backing of the American Indians. At the very least, they wanted to keep them from siding with the British. "Brothers: I am a Warrior," General George Washington said to the Delaware Indians. "My words are few and plain; but I will make good what I say. 'Tis my business to destroy all the Enemies of these States and to protect their friends."[2] Washington tried to make it sound as though the British were weak. He tried to convince the Delaware tribe to back the colonists.

Slave owners always feared that their slaves would rise against them. It was not an idle fear. In South Carolina, for instance, there were far more slaves than non-slaves.[3] Slave rebellions did happen from time to time. In April 1775, just as the war began in New England, three slaves in Virginia were convicted of trying to lead rebellions.[4]

Slave owners across the South feared that the British would provide weapons to help slaves rebel. In the spring of 1775, the Earl of Dunmore, Virginia's royal governor, increased those fears. He revealed a plan "to arm all my own Negroes and receive all others that will come to me whom I shall declare free."[5] A few months later, he declared all slaves free if they would join the British and "bear arms" in the war.[6]

Soon, many slaves were trying to escape to the British side. Some ended up on British ships off the coast of Virginia. Many died there of disease. In Georgia, the British housed two hundred escaped slaves on an island near Savannah. In March 1776, colonists attacked the island. They were aided by some local American Indians. They slaughtered many of the former slaves.[7]

Slaves faced hard decisions. When the British army came near, many fled to join it. Others did not. What if life with the British proved to be no better? What if the British lost the war? Then the slaves would be returned to their angry masters. There were no easy choices.

In the end, thousands of slaves did flee to the British. They still led a hard life. The British often put them to work as blacksmiths, carpenters, or road builders. Sometimes the former slaves were paid for their work. Often they were not. Some were even sent as slaves to islands in the West Indies.[8]

Some African Americans joined the patriot cause. Many of these men were free blacks from the northern colonies. Others were slaves seeking freedom. Many of these slaves did receive their freedom in return for serving in the army.

American Indians found themselves facing the same types of choices. For years, some tribes had done well by trading with the colonists. Others fought with settlers who tried to take their land. Some tribes had learned to play the American colonists and the British against each other. By threatening to support one side or the other, they attempted to make both sides treat them well.

The war made things tougher. Whichever side won would have great power. American Indians wanted to support the side they thought would treat them most fairly. Most tribes believed that side was the British. However, they did not want to back the

American Indians had a difficult time deciding which side to support, but many chose to fight with the British. In this illustration, American Indians and British loyalists defeat a group of American soldiers at the Battle of Wyoming in Pennsylvania on July 3, 1778.

Tribal Alliances

Catawba—backed the colonists

Cherokee—mostly backed the British

Chickasaw—backed the British

Delaware—backed the colonists

Iroquois—mostly backed the British

Seminole—backed the British

losing side. Then they would lose, too. Tribal leaders made choices based on what they thought would be best for their people.

The war split some tribes. For instance, some Cherokee sided with the British. Others wanted to stay neutral.

In the end, most American Indians sided with the British. The British promised to keep settlers out of their lands. The Indians hoped a British victory would protect their way of life.[9]

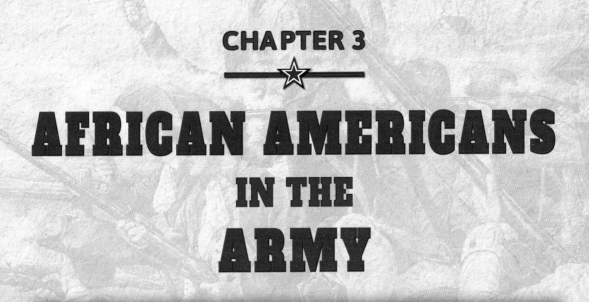

CHAPTER 3
⭐
AFRICAN AMERICANS
IN THE
ARMY

Sleet and snow pelted the Continental soldiers on Christmas night in 1776. General George Washington led his small army across the ice-choked Delaware River in boats. He hoped to launch a surprise attack on the British outpost in Trenton, New Jersey. Helping row Washington's boat was a slave named Prince Whipple. With Whipple's help, Washington got across the river safely. His troops surprised the enemy and won the battle. This triumph helped turn the tide of the war.[1]

A few months earlier, young fifer John Greenwood had seen an African-American soldier wounded in the back of the neck

In this famous painting, Emanuel Leutze dramatizes George Washington's crossing of the Delaware River on December 25, 1776. Prince Whipple, Washington's slave, is one of the men rowing the boat. With Whipple's aid, the boats made it across the river, and the Continental Army scored a major victory at the Battle of Trenton.

Names of Freedom

Many slaves did not have last names. Others were given the last name of their master. Free blacks often took new names. The last names of black soldiers in the Continental Army often showed why they were fighting. One regiment had black soldiers named Jeffrey Liberty, Pomp Liberty, Sharp Liberty, and one with the last name of "Freedom."[2]

at the Battle of Bunker Hill. Blood ran down the man's back. Greenwood asked if the soldier was all right. The man said he was going to get the wound treated. Then he planned to return to the battle. Greenwood said he had been afraid. After seeing that man's bravery, he no longer felt scared.[3]

At first, General Washington did not want black soldiers in the Continental Army. When he took command, Washington issued an order saying that neither "Negroes, boys unable to bear

Successful Spy

James Armistead, a slave, watched as British general Charles Cornwallis moved his army to Yorktown, Virginia. Armistead was a trusted servant to Cornwallis. He pretended to spy for the British. Meanwhile, he was actually spying for the Americans. Armistead informed the Marquis de Lafayette—a French volunteer who served with the Continental Army—of the British army's movements. He provided many important details. In turn, General Lafayette passed the news on to General Washington.

PRIMARY SOURCE

Washington thought he could trap the British troops at Yorktown. He rushed his soldiers south from New York. They were joined by a French fleet. They surrounded Cornwallis and forced him to surrender. That defeat caused the British to give up the war effort.[4]

African-American spy James Armistead stands at right in this 1781 portrait with French General Marquis de Lafayette. Armistead provided Lafayette with important information about British troop movements.

arms, nor old men" were to be enlisted.[5] He feared that white soldiers from the South would refuse to serve with black soldiers. Some southerners feared that giving guns to blacks could lead to a slave uprising.

By the end of 1775, many of the Continental Army volunteers had gone home. The army was shrinking. Washington asked the Continental Congress to decide whether black people could serve. Congress said blacks who were already in the army could reenlist. Many did. Indeed, many black soldiers served for long periods.

A total of about 200,000 men served in the Continental Army or a militia unit during the course of the war.[6] Black soldiers made up only a small part of this number. In all, about 5,000 blacks served. Hundreds of these men were slaves. Many were set free in return for their service.[7]

Others, such as Salem Poor, were freemen. Poor served from 1775 until the end of the war. He suffered through the hard winter at Valley Forge. So did many other black soldiers. In fact, at one point, blacks made up almost 10 percent of Washington's army.[8]

By *his Excellency the Right Honourable* JOHN *Earl of* DUNMORE, *his*

Majefty's Lieutenant and Governour-General of the Colony and Dominion of

Virginia, and Vice-Admiral of the fame:

A PROCLAMATION.

AS I have ever entertained Hopes that an Accommodation might have taken Place between *Great Britain* and this Colony, without being compelled, by my Duty, to this moft difagreeable, but now abfolutely neceffary Step, rendered fo by a Body of armed Men, unlawfully affembled, firing on his Majefty's Tenders, and the Formation of an Army, and that Army now on their March to attack his Majefty's Troops, and deftroy the well-difpofed Subjects of this Colony: To defeat fuch treafonable Purpofes, and that all fuch Traitors, and their Abetters, may be brought to Juftice, and that the Peace and good Order of this Colony may be again reftored, which the ordinary Courfe of the civil Law is unable to effect, I have thought fit to iffue this my Proclamation, hereby declaring, that until the aforefaid good Purpofes can be obtained, I do, in Virtue of the Power and Authority to me given, by his Majefty, determine to execute martial Law, and caufe the fame to be executed throughout this Colony; and to the End that Peace and good Order may the fooner be reftored, I do require every Perfon capable of bearing Arms to refort to his Majefty's S T A N-DARD, or be looked upon as Traitors to his Majefty's Crown and Government, and thereby become liable to the Penalty the Law inflicts upon fuch Offences, fuch as Forfeiture of Life, Confifcation of Lands, &c. &c. And I do hereby farther declare all indented Servants, Negroes, or others (appertaining to Rebels) free, that are able and willing to bear Arms, they joining his Majefty's Troops, as foon as may be, for the more fpeedily reducing this Colony to a proper Senfe of their Duty, to his Majefty's Crown and Dignity. I do farther order, and require, all his Majefty's liege Subjects to retain their Quitrents, or any other Taxes due, or that may become due, in their own Cuftody, till fuch Time as Peace may be again reftored to this at prefent moft unhappy Country, or demanded of them for their former falutary Purpofes, by Officers properly authorifed to receive the fame.

GIVEN *under my Hand, on Board the Ship* William, *off* Norfolk,

the 7th *Day of* November, *in the* 16th *Year of his Majefty's Reign.*

D U N M O R E.

G O D SAVE THE K I N G.

A Copy

Lord Dunmore of Virginia issued this proclamation granting slaves their
freedom if they joined "His Majesty's Troops" to fight for the British cause.

On the other side, many slaves found freedom with the British forces. Some joined units called Black Pioneers. Some former slaves formed their own units. An escaped slave known as Colonel Tye led one such group. He fought in many skirmishes across New Jersey.[9]

In 1775, Lord Dunmore of Virginia invited slaves to join the British. Eight hundred or more slaves did so. Dunmore formed the men into a regiment. In the end, however, he did not lead them into battle. Many died from smallpox. The following summer, Dunmore sent those who remained off to join other British forces.[10]

Many blacks served as sailors. Life aboard the ships was hard. Still, it was better than being a slave. Many colonies had their own navies. In Virginia's navy, at least four African Americans served as pilots. One led an attack on a British ship.[11]

CHAPTER 4

AMERICAN INDIANS IN THE WAR

Smoke rose from burned houses. Crops lay ruined. The summer of 1778 brought war to the Mohawk Valley of New York. First, British and Iroquois Indians defeated the patriot soldiers in the area. Then they attacked American settlers. They burned down houses and barns. In return, patriot patrols burned Indian villages and crops.

The fighting was brutal. Each side accused the other of killing innocent women and children. Most of the claims were false. A few were true. Reports of the fighting caused hatred for the Iroquois among the settlers.[1]

Most American Indians did not want to be drawn into the war between the colonists and the British. Still, the outcome mattered a great deal to them. Many tribes faced the threat of land-hungry settlers.[2]

With this in mind, most American Indians favored the British. Still, many tribes tried to stay out of the fighting as best they could. But in many cases, they could not. War raged all around them. They ended up getting pulled into it. Most American Indians who fought sided with the British. A few fought for the Continental Army.

Leaders in the Continental Congress tried hard to keep the American Indians neutral. They knew how dangerous it would be if large numbers of tribes went to war against them. Virginia governor Patrick Henry pleaded with the colonists to treat the Indians well. "Any Injury done them," he said, "is done to us while they are faithfull."[3]

Still, that was easier said than done. In the lightly settled areas of the north and west, there was frequent fighting between

American Indians and settlers. Many of the battles were vicious. Settlers often destroyed entire Indian villages and farms. Indians burned cabins and mills.[4]

On the western frontier, the British and their Indian allies held the upper hand at first. Then American George Rogers Clark began a daring campaign. He had only two hundred men. Still, he conquered an area twice the size of Great Britain. His small force captured British forts across a wide area. He helped America stake its claim to a huge tract of land. When the war ended, Britain ceded (gave up) this land to the United States.[5]

PRIMARY SOURCE

Charles Willson Peale painted this portrait of Joseph Brant in 1797. The Mohawk chief was named a captain in the British army during the war.

Mohawk Leader

Joseph Brant was a Mohawk leader. As a youth, he had the chance to go to school. There, he learned to speak and write English. For a while, he worked for the British. He helped them in their relations with the Indians. He also translated parts of the Bible into the Mohawk language.

When the American Revolution started, the six tribes of the Iroquois met. The Mohawk were one of these tribes. At first, the tribes voted to stay neutral. Brant later convinced four of the six tribes to support the British. The other two backed the colonists.

During the war, Brant served as head war chief for his tribes. He also was named a captain in the British army. After the war, England gave him a huge tract, or area, of land along the Grand River in Canada. He brought nearly 2,000 Mohawk to live there. The town of Brantford is named after him.[6]

George Rogers Clark (left) accepts the surrender of British Lieutenant Governor Henry Hamilton (right) after the Battle of Vincennes on February 24, 1779. Clark had a very successful campaign in Illinois country against the British and their American Indian allies.

Broken Promise

In 1778, the United States and the Delaware tribe signed a treaty. It contained a remarkable clause. The Delaware agreed to let the American army pass through their lands. They agreed to feed and guide the soldiers. In return, the treaty gave the Delaware tribe the right to have a representative in Congress. In effect, this would have created a new state. Delaware chief White Eyes was pleased with the treaty. There was just one problem. The treaty needed approval from Congress. Congress did not agree to the plan.[7]

To the south, the Cherokee tribe was split apart. The older chiefs wanted peace with the colonists. The young warriors wanted war. They hoped to slow down the spread of white settlers onto their lands. The warriors launched many raids against settlers. Then a force of 6,000 soldiers from four colonies marched out to take revenge. The soldiers were told to "cut up every Indian corn-field, and burn every Indian town."[8]

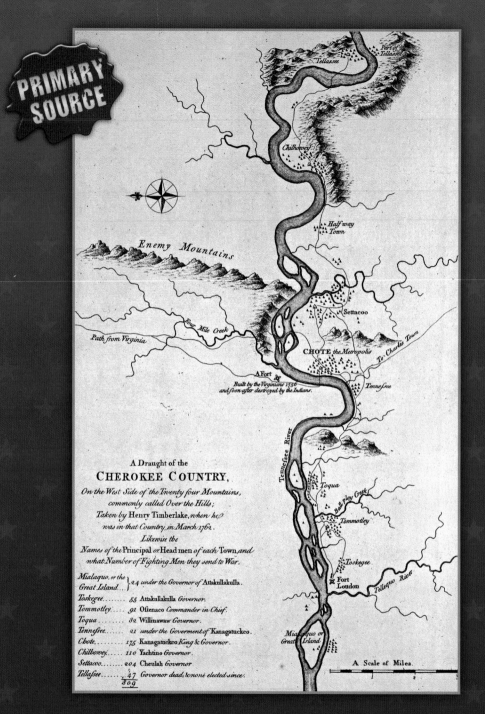

A Draught of the
CHEROKEE COUNTRY,
On the West Side of the Twenty four Mountains,
commonly called Over the Hills;
Taken by Henry Timberlake, when he
was in that Country, in March 1762.

Likewise the
Names of the Principal or Head men of each Town, and
what Number of Fighting Men they send to War.

Mialaquo, or the } 24 under the Governor of Attakullakulla.
Great Island

Toskegee.......... 55 Attakullakulla Governor.
Tommotley........ 91 Ostenaco Commander in Chief.
Toqua............. 82 Willinawaw Governor.
Tennessee......... 21 under the Goverment of Kanagatuckco.
Chote............ 175 Kanagatuckco King & Governor.
Chilhowey........ 110 Yachtino Governor.
Settacoo......... 204 Cheulah Governor.
Tellassee......... 47 Governor dead, & none elected since.
                 ___
                 809

This map shows Cherokee lands near the Little Tennessee River in March
1762. During the Revolution, American soldiers defeated the Cherokee in
battles on the western frontier. After signing treaties with four colonies, the

Within a few months, the Cherokees were beaten. In May 1777, they signed two treaties with four colonies. As a result of these treaties, the Cherokees ceded rights to more than 5 million acres of land. This was an area as big as the state of New Jersey.[9]

For the most part, American Indians suffered as a result of the American Revolution. Many tribes were drawn into the conflict. Others still faced white settlers moving into their lands. After the war, things got even worse for most of the tribes. Settlers streamed west. There was no turning back the tide.

CHAPTER 5

AFTERMATH

The American Revolution brought independence to the United States. It did not bring such benefits to African Americans or American Indians. Slavery continued for eighty more years. In fact, the number of slaves rose from fewer than 500,000 in 1770 to almost 700,000 in 1790.[1]

Some people thought slavery was wrong. Still, most whites continued to view blacks as inferior. Also, slaves were needed to support the economy. Plantation owners in the South especially needed slaves to work on their huge farms.[2]

One by one, northern states passed laws banning slavery. There were few slaves there. Slave labor was not needed to keep the economy running. But even in the north, most whites did not treat blacks as equals.[3]

A few years after the Revolution ended, Congress enacted the Northwest Ordinance. This law outlined how new territories and states would be formed from the western lands won as a result of the war. Slavery was outlawed in these lands. But the U.S. Constitution, which was passed in 1789, protected slavery. It said that the slave trade could not be banned before 1808.[4]

In 1808, Congress did ban the importation of slaves. This meant new slaves could not be brought into the country. The law did not, however, free the slaves who were already in the United States. Slavery remained a problem for decades. In the end, the issue helped lead to the Civil War. The North's victory in that war finally brought slavery to an end.

For American Indians Indians, the American Revolution led to loss. Many lost their lives in battle. Then, after the war, more and more settlers moved west. As a result, many American Indians

The image of a slave in chains appears on this 1837 publication of John Greenleaf Whittier's anti-slavery poem, "Our Countrymen in Chains." Although the United States won its independence during the American Revolution, African-American slaves did not receive their freedom. For many years afterward, abolitionists fought to end slavery. The inhumane institution finally ended with the Thirteenth Amendment to the U.S.

lost their lands and homes. Most tribes had supported the British. When the British lost, they lost, too.

The Treaty of Paris—the treaty between the United States and England to end the American Revolution—did not mention Indians at all. Some British leaders were outraged. They had made treaties with the American Indians. They had tried to preserve Indian land. They thought those treaties should be honored.

Washington and Slavery

George Washington had mixed feelings about using blacks in the army. He knew that they could be good soldiers. He had a black aide named Billy Lee, who served him throughout the war. Washington then gave him his freedom. Still, Washington did not view blacks as equals. He owned more than one hundred slaves.[5]

Washington did treat his slaves well. Over time, his feelings about slavery changed. In his will, he freed all his slaves.[6]

Abolishing Slavery

The Thirteenth Amendment to the U.S. Constitution ended slavery. "Neither slavery nor involuntary servitude . . . shall exist within the United States," it declared. The Thirteenth Amendment was passed by Congress on January 31, 1865. It was ratified, or formally approved, by the states on December 6, 1865.[7]

The Americans disagreed. They had won the war. They believed that allowed them to keep the land the British had controlled. The Treaty of Paris set the boundaries of the United States. Those boundaries extended from Canada in the north to what is now the northern border of Florida in the south, and from the Mississippi River in the west to the Atlantic Ocean in the east. This included many lands that belonged to various Indian tribes. The Americans told the Indians that they had chosen the wrong side in the war. The American Indians could not rely on anyone to protect their rights. They were treated as a conquered people.[8]

Despite the Northwest Ordinance's promise to treat American Indians in "good faith," white settlers continued to push westward onto their lands. This painting shows the Cherokee emigrating to present-day Oklahoma as part of President Andrew Jackson's Indian removal policy in 1838 and 1839. The Cherokee called this forced journey the Trail of Tears.

Congress tried to be fair. In 1787, the Northwest Ordinance set rules about how the western land should be settled. It said that the Indians should be treated with "good faith." It also promised that "their lands and property shall never be taken from them without their consent."[9]

This promise proved empty. Settlers kept pressing westward. Congress could not stop them. Treaties did not stop them. Many tribes fought to save their lands. In some cases, they were able to hold on for a little while. In the end, however, nothing could stop the westward push. For the Indians, the triumph of the American Revolution proved to be the start of a great tragedy.

In all, the American Revolution had brought important changes to many different groups of people. Only time would tell the full impact of those changes.

TIMELINE

Prewar

In 1763, King George III prohibits settlers from moving west of the Appalachian Mountains. This is supposed to prevent conflict between American colonists and American Indians.

During the Boston Massacre of March 5, 1770, Crispus Attucks is shot and killed by British soldiers.

In 1772, a British judge rules that James Sommersett, a slave who escaped while in England, cannot be forced to return to his Virginia master.

1775

In April, the American Revolution begins with fighting at Lexington and Concord, Massachusetts. During the course of the war, some 5,000 African Americans will fight for the patriot cause.

At the Battle of Bunker Hill on June 17, a slave named Peter Salem is believed to have shot Major John Pitcairn as the British officer rallied his men to overrun the American position.

In November, Virginia's royal governor promises freedom to slaves who agree to fight against the rebellious Americans.

1776

In January, Congress approves George Washington's decision to let free blacks reenlist in the Continental Army.

In July, colonial leaders approve the Declaration of Independence. It criticizes King George III for encouraging slave uprisings and attacks against colonists by American Indians, who are referred to as "merciless Indian savages."

1777

In May, the Cherokee tribe signs a pair of peace treaties with four American states. In those treaties, the defeated Cherokees cede 5 million acres of land.

In early summer, a British force that includes hundreds of Indian warriors lays siege to Fort Stanwix, an American post in New York's Mohawk Valley.

1778

More than 700 black Continental soldiers fight alongside their white comrades in the Battle of Monmouth Court House in New Jersey.

Mohawk chief Joseph Brant, an ally of the British, leads Iroquois warriors in a series of raids against American settlers in northern New York.

1779

American generals John Sullivan and James Clinton lead a campaign against the four Iroquois tribes that have allied themselves with the British.

On August 29, 1779, General Sullivan defeats about 1,000 Iroquois warriors in a large battle at Newtown, near present-day Elmira, New York. After the battle, the Americans burn dozens of Indian villages and destroy their crops.

1781–1783

In 1781, slave James Armistead, a patriot spying for the Continental Army, reports that a large British army has moved to Yorktown, Virginia. George Washington decides to try to trap the British there.

British forces at Yorktown surrender on October 19, 1781.

The Treaty of Paris, which officially ends the war, is signed on September 3, 1783. The treaty cedes to the United States a vast expanse of land between the Appalachian Mountains and the Mississippi River.

1787

Congress passes the Northwest Ordinance. It sets up a process for turning new territories in the area into states. Slavery is prohibited in the new lands, and Congress promises to treat American Indians with "good faith."

In September, representatives of the states sign the final draft of the United States Constitution. The document permits the importation of slaves until at least 1808.

CHAPTER NOTES

★

CHAPTER 1: ON THE EVE OF THE REVOLUTION

1. Gary B. Nash, *The Unknown American Revolution: The Unruly Birth of Democracy and the Struggle to Create America* (New York: Viking, 2005), p. 225.
2. Gordon S. Wood, *The American Revolution* (New York: Modern Library, 2002), p. 56.
3. Ray Raphael, *A People's History of the American Revolution: How Common People Shaped the Fight for Independence* (New York: The New Press, 2001), p. 246.
4. "Declaration of Independence," *U.S. History.org*, July 4, 1995, <http://www.ushistory.org/declaration/> (October 16, 2007).
5. Ibid.
6. Dale Taylor, *The Writer's Guide to Everyday Life in Colonial America From 1607–1783* (Cincinnati, Oh.: Writer's Digest Books, 1997), pp. 65–66.
7. Nash, p. 247.

CHAPTER 2: WHICH SIDE TO CHOOSE?

1. "Black Presence, Rights: Slave or Free," *The National Archives* (United Kingdom), n.d., <http://www.nationalarchives.gov.uk/pathways/blackhistory/rights/slave_free.htm> (October 15, 2007).
2. "Speech to the Delaware Chiefs," from "George Washington: A Collection," *The Online Library of Liberty*, <http://oll.libertyfund.org/?option=com_staticxt&staticfile=show.php%Ftitle=848&chapter=101782&layout=html&Itemid=27> (October 15, 2007).
3. Dale Taylor, *The Writer's Guide to Everyday Life in Colonial America From 1607–1783* (Cincinnati, Oh.: Writer's Digest Books, 1997), p. 69.
4. Ray Raphael, *A People's History of the American Revolution: How Common People Shaped the Fight for Independence* (New York: The New Press, 2001), p. 245.
5. Gary B. Nash, *The Unknown American Revolution: The Unruly Birth of Democracy and the Struggle to Create America* (New York: Viking, 2005), p. 160.
6. Alfred W. Blumrosen and Ruth G. Blumrosen, *Slave Nation: How Slavery United the Colonies & Sparked the American Revolution* (Naperville, Ill.: Sourcebooks, Inc., 2005), p. 122.
7. Raphael, p. 261.
8. Ibid., pp. 263–264.
9. John M. Thompson, *The Revolutionary War* (Washington, D.C.: National Geographic Society, 2004), p. 114.

CHAPTER 3: AFRICAN AMERICANS IN THE ARMY

1. Gary B. Nash, *The Unknown American Revolution: The Unruly Birth of Democracy and the Struggle to Create America* (New York: Viking, 2005), p. 225.
2. Thomas Fleming, *Liberty! The American Revolution* (New York: Viking, 1997), p. 151.
3. Bruce Chadwick, *The First American Army: The Untold Story of George Washington and the Men Behind America's First Fight for Freedom* (Naperville, Ill.: Sourcebooks, Inc., 2007), p. 8.
4. Madison Gray, "James Armistead: Patriot Spy," *Time*, n.d., <http://www.time.com/time/2007/blackhistmth/bios/01.html> (February 15, 2008).
5. Fleming, p. 151.
6. Ibid., p. 334.
7. Joseph C. Morton, *The American Revolution* (Westport, Conn.: Greenwood Press, 2003), p. 79.
8. Thomas Fleming, *Washington's Secret War: The Hidden History of Valley Forge* (New York: Smithsonian Books, 2005), pp. 142–143.
9. David Hackett Fischer, *Washington's Crossing* (New York: Oxford University Press, 2004), pp. 160–170.
10. Nash, pp. 162–163.
11. Ray Raphael, *A People's History of the American Revolution: How Common People Shaped the Fight for Independence* (New York: The New Press, 2001), p. 291.

CHAPTER 4: AMERICAN INDIANS IN THE WAR

1. Gary B. Nash, *The Unknown American Revolution: The Unruly Birth of Democracy and the Struggle to Create America* (New York: Viking, 2005), p. 225.
2. Robert Middlekauff, *The Glorious Cause: The American Revolution, 1763–1789* (New York: Oxford University Press, 1982), p. 574.
3. Ray Raphael, *A People's History of the American Revolution: How Common People Shaped the Fight for Independence* (New York: The New Press, 2001), p. 213.
4. John M. Thompson, *The American Revolution* (Washington, D.C.: National Geographic Society, 2004), p. 114.
5. Ibid., pp. 116–117.
6. George L. Marshall, Jr., "Chief Joseph Brant: Mohawk, Loyalist, and Freemason," *Archiving Early America*, 2012, <http://www.earlyamerica.com/review/1998/brant.html> (October 22, 2007).

7. Raphael, pp. 215–216.
8. Ibid., p. 224.
9. Ibid., pp. 226–227.

CHAPTER 5: AFTERMATH

1. Ray Raphael, *A People's History of the American Revolution: How Common People Shaped the Fight for Independence* (New York: The New Press, 2001), p. 296.
2. Robert Middlekauff, *The Glorious Cause: The American Revolution, 1763–1789* (New York: Oxford University Press, 1982), p. 571.
3. Ibid., p. 572.
4. "The Constitution and Slavery," *Constitutional Rights Foundation*, n.d., <http://www.crf-usa.org/lessons/slavery_const.htm> (May 11, 2008).
5. David McCullough, *1776* (New York: Simon & Schuster, 2005), p. 47.
6. Forrest McDonald, "Today's Indispensable Man," in Gary L. Gregg II and Matthew Spalding, eds., *Patriot Sage: George Washington and the American Political Tradition* (Wilmington, Del.: ISI Books, 1999), p. 28.
7. "Primary Source Documents in American History: 13th Amendment to the U.S. Constitution," *Library of Congress*, May 12, 2011, <http://www.loc.gov/rr/program/bib/ourdocs/13thamendment.html> (October 22, 2007).
8. Wilcomb E. Washburn, "Indians and the American Revolution," *American Revolution.org*, n.d., <http://americanrevolution.org/ind1.html> (October 22, 2007).
9. "Text of the Northwest Ordinance," *Archiving Early America*, 2012, <http://www.earlyamerica.com/earlyamerica/milestones/ordinance/text.html> (October 22, 2007).

GLOSSARY

benefit—Something good or helpful; a payment, gift, or other advantage.

brutal—Savage, cruel, or harsh.

cede—To give up; to yield or surrender.

clause—A distinct portion of a formal document, will, or treaty.

convicted—Found guilty of a crime.

enacted—Put into action.

inferior—Lower in place or position; seen as less good.

involuntary—Against one's wishes.

martyr—Someone who dies or suffers to support a cause.

militia—A military unit made up of citizens who are not full-time soldiers but agree to serve in an emergency.

neutral—Not taking sides, especially in an argument or war.

patriot—An American who supported independence from Great Britain during the American Revolution period.

primary source—A document, text, or physical object which was written or created during the time under discussion.

prohibited—Not allowed.

ratified—Formally approved by a governing body, such as Congress.

rebellion—Armed resistance to a government or ruler; resistance to authority.

residents—People who live in a certain place.

servitude—Forced labor or slavery.

skirmishes—Fights between small groups (as opposed to full battles).

tract—An area or piece of land.

uprising—A violent revolt against persons or groups who hold power.

FURTHER READING

⎯⎯★⎯⎯

Books

Blair, Margaret. *Liberty or Death: The Surprising Story of Runaway Slaves Who Sided With the British During the American Revolution.* Washington, D.C.: National Geographic, 2010.

Fleming, Thomas. *Everybody's Revolution: A New Look at the People Who Won America's Freedom.* New York: Scholastic Nonfiction, 2006.

Huey, Lois Miner. *Voices of the American Revolution: Stories From the Battlefields.* Mankato, Minn.: Capstone Press, 2011.

Raatma, Lucia. *African-American Soldiers in the Revolutionary War.* Minneapolis, Minn.: Compass Point Books, 2009.

Internet Addresses

PBS—Africans in America: The Revolutionary War
<http://www.pbs.org/wgbh/aia/part2/2narr4.html>

Liberty!—Chronicle of the Revolution: Joseph Brant & Native Americans
<http://www.pbs.org/ktca/liberty/popup_brant.html>

INDEX